This Book Belongs to:

_____

If found, please return to:

_____

_____

_____

_____

Unicorn Activity Book

Solve cryptograms and create your own

Colour in pictures

Write your own stories using story prompts

Turn your stories into comics

Solve word scrambles

Find word matches

Solve unicorn mazes

Find hidden words in word search puzzles

All the answers are at the back

Cryptograms

These are the most difficult puzzles in the book, but there are some clues to help you.

Cryptograms are special codes, where each letter is substituted for another. For example if A=J. Every A in the cryptogram is then replaced by J.

Each cryptogram is related to unicorns and there are picture clues for each one. You can also colour in the pictures.

If you can't solve the cryptogram with the help of the pictures, look on the back of the pictures to find the code for one of the letters.

Then you can look at the cryptogram to see how many times that letter is there. There are also six grids with all the letters of the alphabet and boxes to fill in the code. You can use the grid to help you work out the letters. Use pencil in case you make mistakes!

Each cryptogram uses a DIFFERENT code.

CRYPTOGRAMS

1. LAX BAPUTEXZ OXREBAXT CME LAX JZPBMEZ..

2. DZNK TANQSLA NK HWMMNAB.

USE A PENCIL TO TRY TO WORK OUT THE CODE FOR ONE OF THE CRYPTOGRAMS. YOU CAN RUB IT OUT AND TRY AGAIN IF YOU MAKE A MISTAKE!

A	B	C	D	E	F	G	H
I	J	K	L	M	N	O	P
Q	R	S	T	U	V	W	X
Y	Z						

CLUES TO CRYPTOGRAM #1
ANOTHER CLUE ON THE BACK!

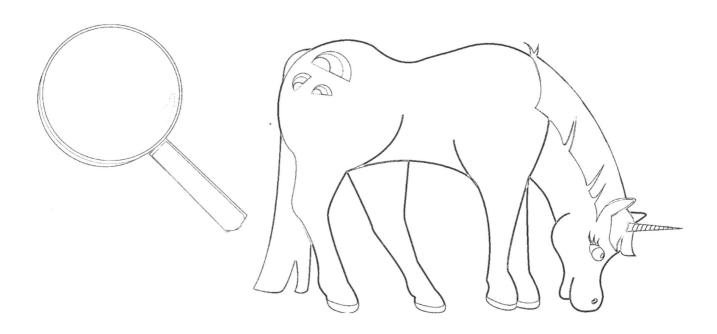

Clue

In Cryptogram #1,

A=H

CLUE TO CRYPTOGRAM #2

ANOTHER CLUE ON THE BACK!

CLUE

In Cryptogram #2

A=N

USE A PENCIL TO TRY TO WORK OUT THE CODE FOR ONE OF THE CRYPTOGRAMS

A	B	C	D	E	F	G	H
I	J	K	L	M	N	O	P
Q	R	S	T	U	V	W	X
Y	Z						

CRYPTOGRAMS

3. CRALL YSUAO HSJPMASV.

4. LU LA DXLZLZV WZLFHDZ USXDA.

CLUE TO CRYPTOGRAM #3   ANOTHER CLUE ON THE BACK!

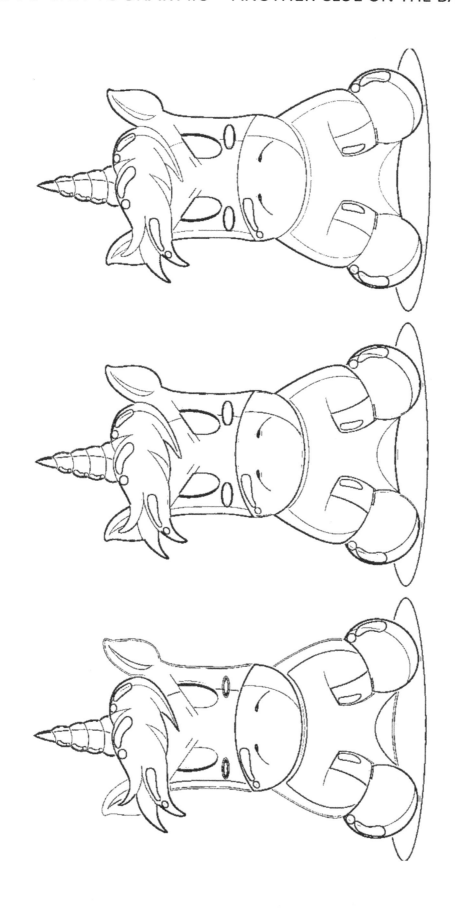

CLUE

In Cryptogram #3

A=R

USE A PENCIL TO TRY TO WORK OUT THE CODE
FOR ONE OF THE CRYPTOGRAMS

A	B	C	D	E	F	G	H
I	J	K	L	M	N	O	P
Q	R	S	T	U	V	W	X
Y	Z						

USE A PENCIL TO TRY TO WORK OUT THE CODE FOR ONE OF THE CRYPTOGRAMS

A	B	C	D	E	F	G	H
I	J	K	L	M	N	O	P
Q	R	S	T	U	V	W	X
Y	Z						

CLUES TO CRYPTOGRAM #4

ANOTHER CLUE ON THE BACK!

CLUE

In Cryptogram #4

Z=N

USE A PENCIL TO TRY TO WORK OUT THE CODE FOR ONE OF THE CRYPTOGRAMS. YOU CAN RUB IT OUT AND TRY AGAIN IF YOU MAKE A MISTAKE!

A	B	C	D	E	F	G	H
I	J	K	L	M	N	O	P
Q	R	S	T	U	V	W	X
Y	Z						

CRYPTOGRAMS

5. IDAN TAIITC MABT AN RBCNNCR EN E VWAFUBW..

6. BDEH ZNB EH BXFELC DNXW BM RI N TLEZMXL..

CLUE TO CRYPTOGRAM #5
ANOTHER CLUE ON THE BACK!

CLUE

In Cryptogram #5

N=S

USE A PENCIL TO TRY TO WORK OUT THE CODE FOR ONE OF THE CRYPTOGRAMS. YOU CAN RUB IT OUT AND TRY AGAIN IF YOU MAKE A MISTAKE!

A	B	C	D	E	F	G	H
I	J	K	L	M	N	O	P
Q	R	S	T	U	V	W	X
Y	Z						

Try writing a new message with one or more of the cryptogram codes you have deciphered.

CLUE TO CRYPTOGRAM #6 ANOTHER CLUE ON THE BACK!

CLUE

In Cryptogram #6

B=T

Try writing a new message with one or more of the cryptogram codes you have deciphered.

MAKE YOUR OWN CODE FOR CRYPTOGRAMS

A	B	C	D	E	F	G	H
I	J	K	L	M	N	O	P
Q	R	S	T	U	V	W	X
Y	Z						

Write messages using your own cryptogram code.

MAKE ANOTHER CODE FOR CRYPTOGRAMS

A	B	C	D	E	F	G	H
I	J	K	L	M	N	O	P
Q	R	S	T	U	V	W	X
Y	Z						

Write messages using your own cryptogram code.

MAKE ANOTHER CODE FOR CRYPTOGRAMS

A	B	C	D	E	F	G	H
I	J	K	L	M	N	O	P
Q	R	S	T	U	V	W	X
Y	Z						

Write messages using your cryptogram code.

MAKE ANOTHER CODE FOR CRYPTOGRAMS

A	B	C	D	E	F	G	H
I	J	K	L	M	N	O	P
Q	R	S	T	U	V	W	X
Y	Z						

Write messages using your cryptogram code.

MAKE ANOTHER CODE FOR CRYPTOGRAMS

A	B	C	D	E	F	G	H
I	J	K	L	M	N	O	P
Q	R	S	T	U	V	W	X
Y	Z						

Write messages using your cryptogram code.

Write messages using your cryptogram code.

Stories and Comics

Write your own stories, using the prompts as a starting point. Then turn each story into a comic, using the storyboard pages to draw the main events.

Use your imagination to create exciting adventures and your own superheroes – or be the superhero in your story!

There are two lined pages for the story and four comic style pages for your drawings.

The children were staying with their grandparents at the edge of the magical forest. They were hoping to see the unicorn who came out every night. One night, there was a huge storm.

The youngest unicorn started playing with the baby foxes and suddenly he realised that his family had gone and he was lost in the mountains.

We were all sitting round the campfire, when we suddenly saw a bright light streaking across the sky. Could it be the unicorn that was said to live here?

The little girl was very lonely and so she pretended that she had a friend who was a unicorn. Then one day . . ..

The young unicorns decided to leave home so that they could have a big adventure.

At Halloween, the witch promised the twins that they could fly with her to the place where the unicorn lives..

My Ideas for Stories and Comics

Word Searches

The words at the bottom of the page are hidden in the puzzle above. Sometimes they go backwards or diagonally and they can go from bottom to top.

UNICORN WORDSEARCH #1

```
D B I C T Y L L T L O A H J R
A Y M E N C K A D N G B M G S
T F W T N O Q K C N T A T C P
O Z U D F K X C W I Z A R D N
K D I I V T N K E G G W Q Z T
A U N G E V B T L W K A Z V B
E N M E M R T X S T M L M L U
H I I U D Q A S B E M X A T J
J C X M O D A E O H R Y P I C
A O H S A C I N S P T O V H H
E R H O W L S H H C H H F Q Y
K N W B G J S W H U J Z S J E
T O H Q X S Q I S I R V B N O
A G Y K C E D F S I R B U I B
J U R T R B W T A L J X M S K
```

ANIMALS   FOREST   HIDDEN
MAGICAL   UNICORN   WIZARD

UNICORN WORDSEARCH #2

```
Y F X T B U O H H Z L I C Y M
R S H B S Z M I I B E S R J Z
D I A Q W K R P K Q L Y H X I
G R P T I I A A Q Q P X B V Z
E Y P P N M E T P H D T V M S
M O I J S A A D D I J O S B G
S C N C P G F G U O G O T D S
V L E D I I V K G J G J V C M
Y X S O R N T D J E M V D L O
D V S Z E A X W S E D S I N H
C S T B G T O S P G U A D R L
S W O B N I A R F B H Q K Y C
I Y L E A O L R G N A Q E U Y
T A G S G N I W R R U U V W E
N X H R U L J D R M K C N I J
```

FANTASY   HAPPINESS   IMAGINATION
INSPIRE   RAINBOWS   WINGS

Word Scrambles

The letters on the left make a word related in some way to unicorns, but they are scrambled.

Unscramble them to find the word.

WORD SCRAMBLE #1

ERTSFO   _ _ _ _ _ _

NSLAAIM   _ _ _ _ _ _ _

GIWSN   _ _ _ _ _

IWRSHPE   _ _ _ _ _ _ _

EIATLFUBU   _ _ _ _ _ _ _ _ _

ARDEM   _ _ _ _ _

WORD SCRAMBLE #2

ARFEODEH   _ _ _ _ _ _ _

OREDNH   _ _ _ _ _ _

LCRAUFEG   _ _ _ _ _ _ _ _

EDNAC   _ _ _ _ _

ERRTECAU   _ _ _ _ _ _ _ _

SNUAULU   _ _ _ _ _ _ _

Word Matches

The words on the left go with one of the words on the right. Find the words that are the best match for each other.

Sometimes the words mean the same thing and sometimes they are related to each other.

UNICORN WORD MATCH #1

unicorn	trees
forest	sleep
flying	creature
rainbow	wings
dream	storm

UNICORN WORD MATCH #2

story	insect
horse	unbelievable
thunder	animal
butterfly	moondust
sparkle	book
magical	lightning

Mazes

Start each maze at the S near the top and trace your way to the E without crossing any lines.

Maze #1

Start at S

End at E

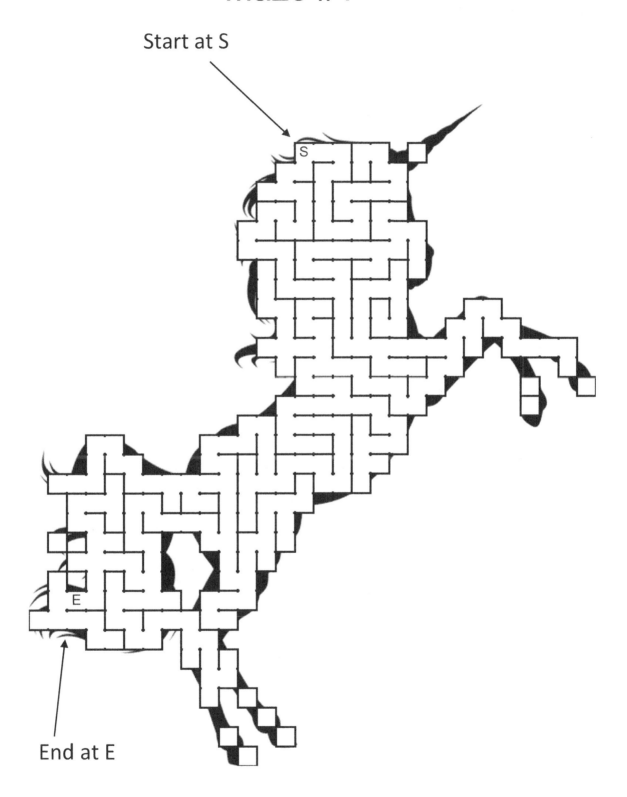

Maze #2

Start at S

End at E

Maze #3

Start at S

End at E

Maze #4

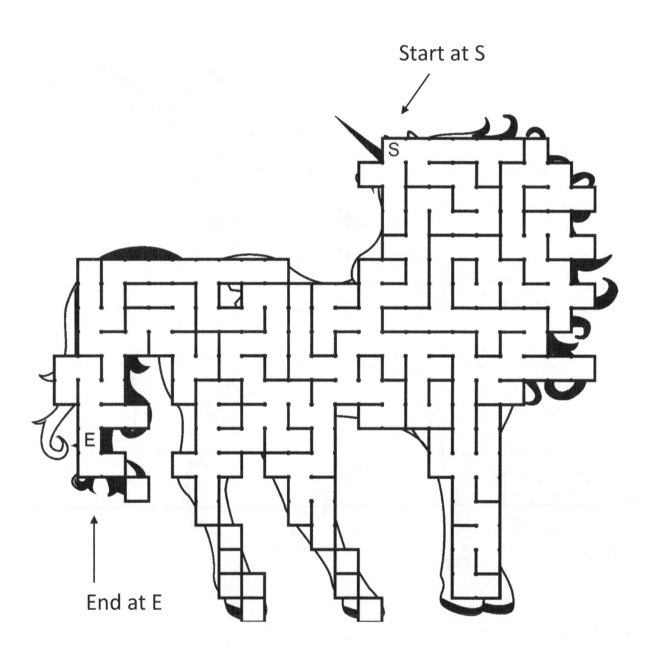

Maze #5

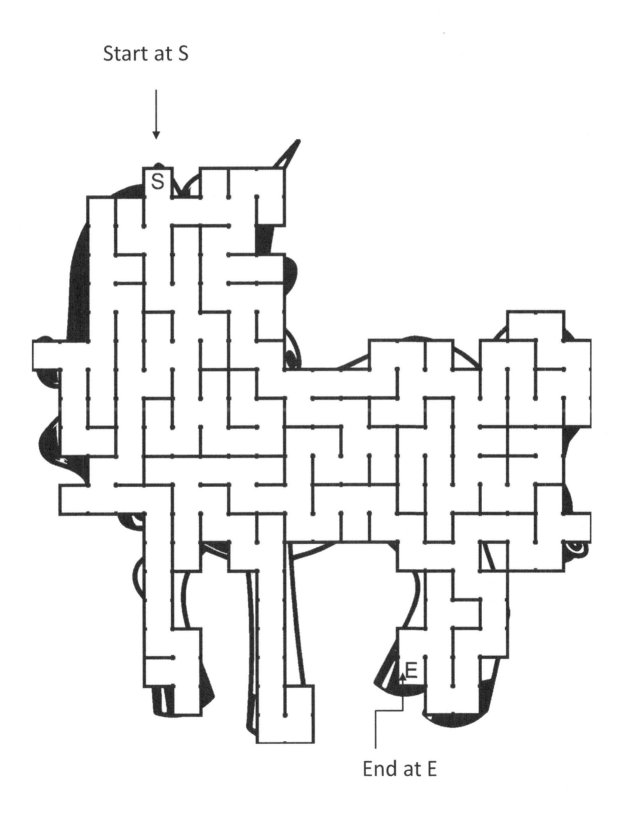

SOLUTIONS

ANSWERS TO THE CRYPTOGRAMS

1. The children searched for the unicorn.

2. This unicorn is dabbing.

3. Three angry unicorns.

4. It is raining unicorn tears.

5. This little girl is dressed as a unicorn..

6. This cat is trying hard to be a unicorn..

WORD SCRAMBLE #1

ERTSFO = FOREST

NSLAAIM = ANIMALS

GIWSN = WINGS

IWRSHPE = WHISPER

EIATLFUBU = BEAUTIFUL

ARDEM = DREAM

WORD SCRAMBLE #2

ARFEODEH = FOREHEAD

OREDNH = HORNED

LCRAUFEG = GRACEFUL

EDNAC = DANCE

ERRTECAU = CREATURE

SNUAULU = UNUSUAL

WORD SEARCH #1

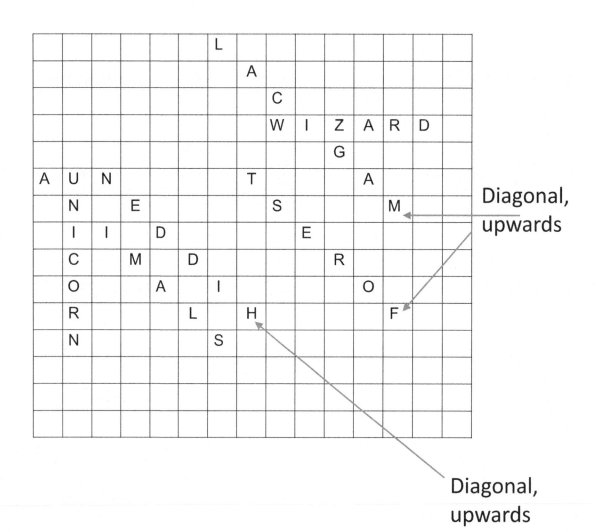

WORD SEARCH #2

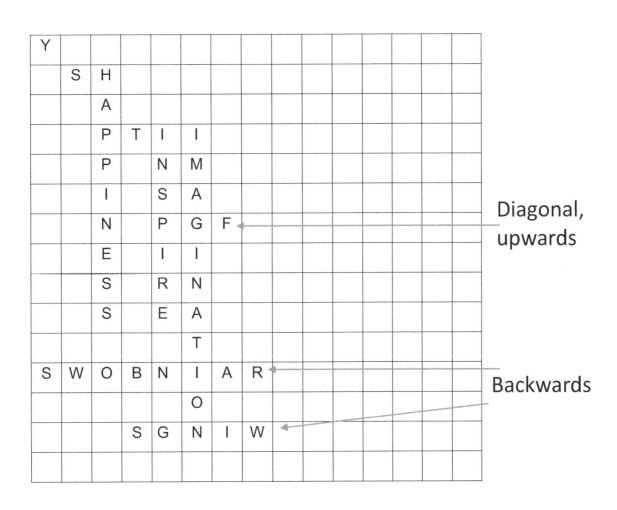

WORD MATCH #1

unicorn = creature

forest = trees

flying = wings

rainbow = storm

dream = sleep

WORD MATCH #2

story = book

horse = animal

thunder = lightning

butterfly = insect

sparkle = moondust

magical = unbelievable

Solution to Maze #1

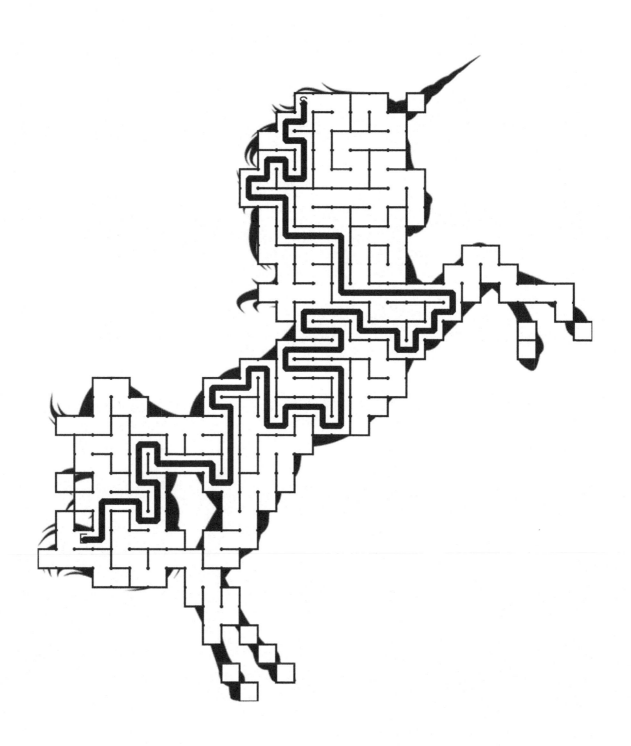

Solution to Maze #2

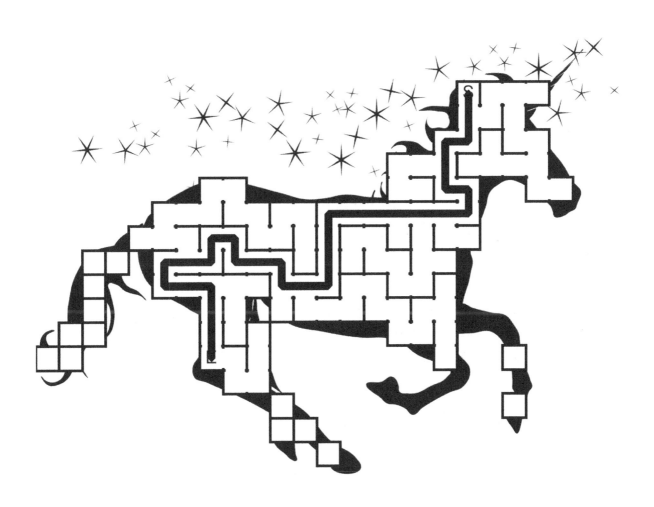

Solution to Maze #3

Solution to Maze #4

Solution to Maze #5

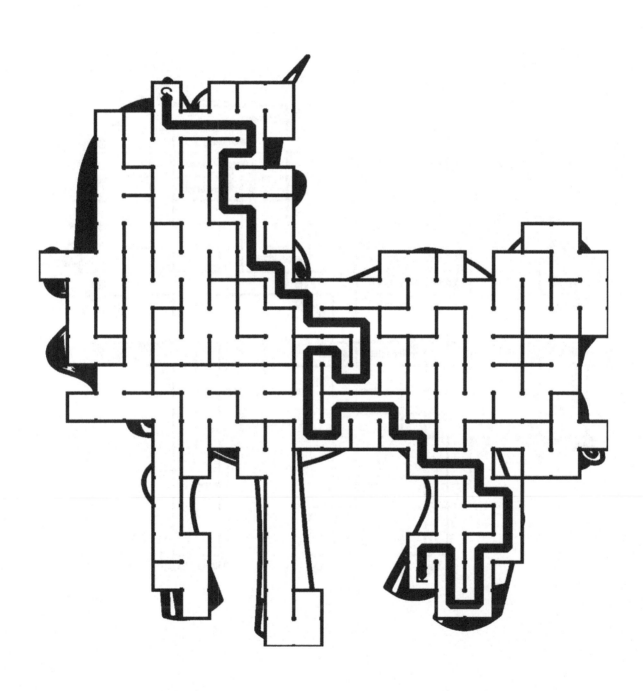

Made in the USA
Monee, IL
02 April 2020